If you purchas be aware that reported as "u the author has not received payment for this "stripped book."

I AM SOLUTIONS PUBLISHING.

A TRANSFORMATIVE JOURNEY FROM POTENTIAL TO PURPOSE

by

Andre S. Butler

ISBN (Hardcover): 978-2-7841-5775-0

ISBN (Paperback): 978-2-8787-0428-0

ISBN (Ebook): 978-2-0160-5989-0

Order Form

For more information or wholesale requests, write:
Levitical Communications Inc.
P.O. Box 1324 - Bear, DE 19701

Check all that apply:

Title	Cost	Qty
❑ Israelites and Jews	$15.00	______
❑ Final Resolution	$17.00	______

Please send me the book(s) checked above at the total cost of $________.
Add $4.75 for shipping and handling (add $. 75 for each additional book).

Name: ____

Address: ____

City State, Zipcode: ____

Please complete the form above, include the proper funds and mail to:
Levitical Communications Inc.
P.O. Box 1324 - Bear, DE 19701

For Credit Card Orders VISA, MASTERCARD, DISCOVER
or AMERICAN EXPRESS call (202) 291-0050.

Acknowledgments

First and foremost, I want to give all glory and honor to God, the Creator of every opportunity, the Author of my purpose, and the Sustainer of my journey. Without His divine guidance, grace, and unfailing love, this book—and the life that has led to it—would not have been possible.

Every word written is a testament to His faithfulness and the purpose He has instilled within me. Thank you, Lord, for choosing me to be a vessel for Your work.

To my incredible wife, Torri Butler—words cannot fully express my gratitude for you. You are not just my partner in life, but my anchor, my confidante, and my greatest supporter. Your unwavering love, patience, and encouragement have given me the strength to pursue my calling, even when the journey seemed impossible. You inspire me daily with your resilience, wisdom, and grace, and I am profoundly grateful to walk this path with you by my side.

To my six beautiful children—Diella, Leilani, Judah, Josiah, Lion, and Arabella—you are the light of my life and my greatest joy. Each of you brings a unique spirit into our family, and I am blessed beyond measure to be your father. Thank you for teaching me the true meaning of love, patience, and purpose. Your laughter, curiosity, and boundless energy inspire me to be the best version of myself.

To my mom, Sonja—your constant support, unwavering belief in me, and endless prayers have been a guiding light in my life. You have been my rock, always there to lift me up when I needed it most.

To my mom, Nicole—I owe so much of who I am to you. You raised me and shaped the foundation of my life. I would not be the person I am today without your influence. You were there through every high and low, and your unwavering support has meant more to me than words can express. Thank you!

A special acknowledgment to my dad, Andre Butler Senior—Dad, your wisdom, guidance, and example have been pivotal in shaping me into the man I am today. You've taught me the value of hard work, integrity, and perseverance. Your influence runs deep in every aspect of my life, and I am eternally grateful for the lessons you've imparted and the love you've shown.

To all my mentors over the years—each of you has played a significant role in my personal and professional growth. Your insights, wisdom, and guidance have been invaluable, and I carry the lessons you've taught me in every endeavor I pursue. Thank you for believing in me, challenging me, and helping me grow.

Lastly, but certainly not least, to everyone who has supported me, believed in me, and prayed for me throughout this journey—thank you. This book is as much yours as it is mine, and I am deeply grateful for each and every one of you.

Thank you all for being a part of this incredible journey with me.

Contents

About The Author

Andre Butler is an author, international speaker, and spiritual father to the next generation. As a senior leader of The Well Global in Miami, Florida, and founder of The Disciple and Nexgen Up, Andre has helped thousands of people over the last 15 years put fear-based limitations behind them, overcome obstacles, and hone in on their true goals and purpose so they can reach their destiny.

Andre has a diverse background in business, counseling, consulting, pastoring, and teaching, which gives him unique leadership insights and perspectives.

Andre lives in beautiful Homestead, Florida with his wife, Torri, and their six children. When home, you can find Andre, writing, reading, singing, or watching movies.

Foreword

In a world filled with distractions and detours, finding our purpose can often feel like searching for a needle in a haystack. But what if I told you that the key to unlocking your limitless purpose lies within the pages of this book?

"The Journey from Potential to Purpose" by Andre Butler is not just another self-help book; it is a transformative guide that will revolutionize the way you view your life's journey. With practical insights and profound wisdom, Butler illuminates the path from mere potential to a life of purpose-driven fulfillment.

Imagine standing in the middle of a vast field, surrounded by tall grasses that seem to stretch on endlessly. You know that somewhere in this field lies a needle, but finding it seems like an impossible task. This is how many of us feel when it comes to finding our purpose in life. We know it's out there somewhere, but the path to discovering it is shrouded in uncertainty and confusion.

But what if I told you that the needle is not actually lost? What if I told you that it is right there in front of you, waiting to be found? "The Journey from Potential to Purpose" is like a map that will guide you through the field, helping you navigate the twists and turns until you finally uncover the needle that has been there all along.

Too many individuals today feel like they have failed in fulfilling their purpose. They wander through life, feeling lost and unfulfilled, unaware of the untapped potential that lies within them. Andre Butler's book is a beacon of hope for those who are struggling to find their way. It provides a roadmap for self-discovery, igniting the fire within each of us to pursue our true calling.

Imagine waking up every morning with a sense of clarity and purpose, knowing exactly what you need to do to make a meaningful impact on the world. This is the promise of "The Journey from Potential to Purpose." It is not just a book; it is a transformational tool that will guide you on a journey of self-discovery and empowerment.

Through his book, Butler unveils the eight keys that will not only help you cut your time in half but also reveal the purpose of your journey. These keys are like stepping stones that will guide you across the river of uncertainty, helping you reach the other side where your purpose awaits.

One of the most powerful aspects of Butler's book is the way it encourages readers to shift their perspective. Instead of viewing their lives as a series of random events, Butler encourages readers to see their lives as a journey toward purpose. This shift in perspective can be life-changing, as it allows individuals to see the challenges and setbacks they face as opportunities for growth and development.

If you are feeling like you are failing on purpose, if you are feeling purposely bankrupt and unfulfilled, then this book is your cheat code. It is your GPS to finding and fulfilling your God-given purpose.

I believe that the richest place in the world isn't in the graveyard of men but in the minds of individuals who are alive but dead to their purpose. Let Andre Butler's book breathe new life into your purpose and unlock the wonders that await you on your journey from potential to purpose.

Guidelines For Transformation

To ensure you get the most out of "Unveiling the Blueprint" and truly unlock your potential, it's important to approach this book as a guide, not just a read. The transformative journey from potential to purpose requires more than passive reading; it demands active engagement and intentional action. Here's how to maximize your experience and achieve lasting change:

How to Use This Book for Maximum Impact

1. Commit to the Journey:
This book is designed to be more than just informative; it's meant to be transformational. Commit to fully engaging with the content, knowing that each chapter is a step toward uncovering and living out your divine purpose.

2. Active Participation:
Don't just read—participate. At the end of each chapter, you'll find reflection questions and actionable steps. These are not optional; they're crucial for your growth. Take the time to answer the questions thoughtfully and apply the steps consistently.

3. Journaling and Reflection:
Keep a journal as you progress through the book. Write down your thoughts, reflections, and any insights you gain. This practice will help solidify your understanding and allow you to track your growth over time.

4. Set Realistic Goals:
As you uncover your dreams and set goals, make sure they're realistic and achievable. Break down larger goals into smaller, actionable steps, and set deadlines to keep yourself accountable.

5. Take Your Time:

This journey is not a race. Take your time with each chapter, allowing the lessons and insights to sink in. Don't rush through the exercises; give them the attention they deserve.

6. Seek Accountability:

Share your journey with a trusted friend, mentor, or accountability partner. Discuss your goals, challenges, and progress. Having someone to encourage and hold you accountable can make a significant difference.

7. Apply and Reflect:

Application is key. Make a conscious effort to apply the principles and strategies you learn in your daily life. Reflect regularly on how these changes are impacting your life and what adjustments you might need to make.

8. Be Open to Change:
Be open to the changes this journey may bring. Embrace the process of growth, even when it challenges you. Remember, transformation often requires stepping out of your comfort zone.

9. Revisit and Reassess:
Periodically revisit previous chapters and your journal entries. Assess your progress, celebrate your wins, and identify areas for further improvement. Growth is an ongoing process, and revisiting concepts can deepen your understanding.

10. Pray and Seek Guidance:
Throughout this journey, seek divine guidance. Pray for clarity, strength, and wisdom as you pursue your purpose. Allow your faith to be your anchor, guiding you through each step.

This book is a tool, but the real power lies in your willingness to apply what you learn. Transformation comes from consistent, intentional action. As you journey from potential to purpose, remember that the process is unique to you. Embrace the journey, stay committed, and trust that the steps you take today will lead you to a life of greater purpose and fulfillment.

By engaging deeply with "Unveiling the Blueprint", you're not just discovering your purpose; you're preparing to live it out fully. Let this book be your guide as you step into the life you were always meant to live.

Introduction

Welcome to a journey unlike any other—a journey from potential to purpose. This book is not just a collection of ideas and experiences; it is a map designed to guide you through the complexities of life, helping you uncover and activate the vast reservoir of potential within you.

The Journey Begins

Every person is born with an inherent potential, a seed of greatness waiting to be nurtured and brought to fruition. Yet, too often, this potential remains untapped, buried under layers of fear, doubt, and limiting beliefs. The journey from potential to purpose is a transformative process, requiring courage, commitment, and a deep understanding of oneself.

My own journey began in the most unexpected place—on the battlefield in Iraq. Facing death brought a clarity and urgency that changed my life forever. It was in that moment, with a bomb landing nearby, that I realized how fleeting life can be. I didn't want to leave this world full of unfulfilled potential. I wanted to die empty, having poured out all that I was created to be.

From that moment, my quest to discover my purpose became a relentless pursuit. I sought guidance from mentors, faced numerous obstacles, and learned invaluable lessons along the way. This book is a culmination of those experiences, designed to help you navigate your own path from potential to purpose.

Throughout this journey, you will encounter various enemies that seek to hinder your progress. Fear, comparison, and excuses are some of the most formidable foes you will face. In this book, we will explore how to recognize and overcome these enemies, drawing from both my experiences and timeless wisdom.

One of the most critical elements of this journey is understanding your 'why.' Your 'why' is the driving force that keeps you moving forward, even when the road gets tough. It is the source of your motivation and the foundation of your resilience. We will delve into the importance of having a strong 'why' and how it can transform your journey.

Your Journey Awaits

The journey from potential to purpose is deeply personal and unique to each individual. It requires introspection, dedication, and a willingness to grow. But the rewards are immeasurable. As you embark on this journey, remember that you are not alone. You have a higher power guiding you, a community of support, and a purpose waiting to be discovered and fulfilled.

This book is your guide, your map, and your companion on this incredible journey. It is filled with practical insights, inspiring stories, and powerful tools to help you unlock your potential and live your purpose.

Are you ready to embark on this journey? Are you ready to uncover the buried treasure within you and let it shine for the world to see? If so, let's begin this transformative adventure together. The world is waiting for you to step into your destiny.

It's time to unlock your potential and live your purpose.

THE JOURNEY FROM POTENTIAL TO PURPOSE

1
The Richest Place In The World

Potential... That is an interesting word. Everything and everybody has it. Every single person was born with this amazing gift called potential. It's a word filled with promise, yet often overlooked within us all. Within each person lies a reservoir of untapped ability, waiting to be harnessed for a purpose greater than ourselves. It is the seed of greatness, the spark of divine creativity bestowed upon each of us. Everything in life begins as potential. Which is why many people are searching to answer this one question. A question that I believe is the most important question in the world. Why? Because this question leads to the most important answer in the world.

Why Am I Here?

Amidst life's uncertainties, this question resonates deeply, inviting us to explore our unique calling and destiny. Our lives are not accidents but deliberate creations; each of us is crafted with intentionality and endowed with gifts meant to impact the world.

Have you ever wondered why you were created? What are you supposed to be doing? What is your purpose? I have asked myself that question many times. The unfortunate thing is many people will never get the opportunity to answer that question and will die full of untapped potential and purpose.

> *"The greatest tragedy in life is not death, but a life without a purpose."* - Myles Monroe

As a young boy, I attended a conference in the Bahamas. There were many speakers there and thousands of people. I remember sitting there just listening to these men and women speak on many different subjects. But then I heard some words that one day came back and saved my life. Dr. Myles Munroe said that the richest place in the world is the cemetery because of all the potential that never became a reality. I didn't really understand it then, but years later and thousands of miles from home, those powerful keywords that he spoke suddenly came out of my memory. In a moment when I faced death, he saved my life with those words. What happened to me? How did I get to that moment?

Well, it actually starts with a love story. I met the girl of my dreams, Torri Butler and we had just got married. It was back in October 2008. The country was weeks away from electing its 44th president, a new Commander in Chief. I was in the military at the time, having joined the Air Force as a young man. I was only 22 years old, and I couldn't be happier. Torri was the type of girl you bring home to your parents. Like, they were proud that I got a good one. I was proud, too. She and I were about to start our new lives together. We'd gotten married in Florida and I wanted to take her to see and meet my family in Philadelphia, Pennsylvania. But then the plane landed at the Philadelphia airport, and that's when I got the call to serve this great country. Torri and I hadn't even gotten off the plane. I turned my phone on, and that's when it rang. I was surprised to hear the voice of my boss, Sergeant Brown, on the other end of the phone. What he said next I have never forgotten. He told me I needed to turn around and go back to Eglin Air Force Base, just outside of Valparaiso, Florida, because I was deploying to Iraq.

Even thinking about it now makes my heart drop. I can't describe how sad I became in that moment. With incredible sorrow, I had to tell my beautiful, brand-new wife, Torri, who was sitting in the airplane seat next to me, that I had to go. Honestly, the only thing I could think about was dying. I didn't want to die and I didn't want to leave my wife. I just kept thinking about how tragic it would be to die. Before I knew it, I was on that long, awful 30-hour flight to Iraq. Many things went through my mind as we traveled. I was young, newly married, and scared.

After landing in Iraq, we got our briefing. I barely had time to catch my breath and recover from flying over several time zones and so many thousands of miles, when we were suddenly bombed. Only fifteen minutes after the briefing - Bomb after bomb after bomb. It really was a war zone, and not like you ever see in the movies. This was so loud, and it shook my body with every blast. Our base was targeted, and as we all hid for cover, all I could think about was my wife and how I didn't want to die. If you can believe it, the bombing became the norm. My daily life soon was filled with at least six or seven bombs.

I didn't know it then, but my life was about to change, and not in a way I could have ever expected or predicted. I was just sitting in my truck watching some of the local nationals on base, another typical day in Iraq. Yet again, we started getting bombed. As bomb after bomb went off, booming all around us, we ran for cover. Suddenly, a bomb landed right in front of me – and it didn't go off.

At that moment, it just hit me, in such a powerful way I was shaken. My life not only flashed before my eyes, but everything I've ever thought about became clear. One thing immediately jumped into my mind. I was thinking about what Dr. Munroe had said, years earlier to me:

"The richest place in the world is the cemetery."

Well, before Iraq, I never truly understood that before. But, it made total sense in that moment.

The cemetery is full of books that were never written, inventions that were never invented, and music that was never composed or created. In the cemetery is so much potential that never became a reality. And as I stood there, in Iraq, two feet away from death, I also realized there was something more tragic than death:

A life without purpose.

I survived Iraq, and I came home. I was forever changed and will never forget my experience ever again! I worked to find my purpose and discovered it's only part of a greater journey. A journey that you can take along with me. Let's go together.

I want you to journey with me because I want you to answer your question about purpose. Many people never get the opportunity to answer that question. Instead, they end up dying completely full. They're full of dreams, passions, and potential that never became a reality. But, what happens when you live a life of purpose? You release everything inside of you. You share it with your family, with your friends, with your community, and with the world at large. You enrich your life, you touch others' lives, and you become empty because you have shared your value.

How will you die: FULL or EMPTY?

"It's more tragic to be alive and not know why, than to be dead and not know life." - Myles Munroe

How do you release everything inside of you, so that you are able to die empty – and avoid the tragedy of not knowing what you are here for?

What are you releasing that's inside of you?

In all of us is a treasure we can give the world. When Dr. Myles Munroe said, "The richest place in the world is the cemetery," he was talking about this same buried treasure.

Do you believe that you have this treasure inside of you? It's true. Every person in your life, including yourself, is walking around with this treasure inside of them. Yes, it really is there. You have it with you every day. It's invisible, but it can be one of the most powerful things you've ever thought about in your life. Everyone has it, but they don't know how to activate it. They don't know how to unlock it.

This buried treasure is made up of precious wealth that is more valuable than gold, silver, and jewels. It's made up of the dreams that you still carry and the ideas that you haven't taken any action on yet. There's another word for this untapped wealth within you:

Potential

That's what is buried in you and every cemetery in the world. It's potential, a treasure that will not just enrich you, but enrich the world, too.

It's how far you can go, but you haven't gone there yet.

Think of all the astonishing things people have done with their gifts, talents, abilities, and perseverance. Every building that you've ever seen, every book you've ever read, every piece of music you've listened to – they were all created because that person took the first step to unlock the treasure of their potential. Yes, every person who's ever inspired you had the same treasure that you have. A doctor started off with potential and is now saving lives. An author started out with potential and is now changing lives. A coach started out with potential and is now developing lives to their fullest. But it's not just others who will be impacted by you unlocking and tapping into your potential. You will gain things that you might have wanted for a long time, but can now gain as rewards along the journey. Things like confidence, focus, drive, fulfillment, success, and significance.

Potential is truly an awesome thing. But, it requires you to activate it. Just like a video game just sits there, waiting for you to play it, and waiting for you to join. That is how potential is. It's sitting there inside of you until it becomes activated. If you never activate it, you will never find your purpose, you will never have a purpose, and you will never get the energy to work towards it. Potential is full of possibilities. All it needs is a direction to go and an end goal to shoot for.

May this journey inspire you to embrace the fullness of your potential, to unearth the treasures buried within, and to live each day with unwavering faith in God's guiding hand. Let us embark on this quest together, daring to uncover the mysteries of purpose and destiny, and to live a life that echoes in eternity.

CHAPTER ONE

The Richest Place In The World

The greatest tragedy in life is not death, but a life without a purpose.
-Dr Myles Monroe

Summary

What dreams and talents have you yet to explore?

So now that you know what potential is, how do you release it? Have you had your near-death experience to make you question your purpose in life? The unfortunate thing is some people don't get a second chance to start seeking out their purpose, but you have the opportunity right now to make that happen. Why risk losing your life before you've truly lived it?

Reflection

Reflect on the potential within you that remains untapped. What dreams and talents have you yet to explore? Consider the impact you want to have on the world and the legacy you wish to leave behind.

Actionable Steps:

It's time to take action!

1. **Reflect on Untapped Potential:** Identify areas in your life where potential lies dormant. Consider the dreams and aspirations you've neglected.

2. **Set an Intention:** Write down one area of your life where you want to activate potential and set an intention to explore it further.

3. **Create a Vision Statement:** Write a personal vision statement that captures your desires and potential, serving as a guide for future decisions.

4. **Identify Role Models:** Research and list people who have realized similar potential or dreams. Analyze their journeys for inspiration and guidance.

Guided Exercise:

Journal Prompt: Spend 10 minutes journaling about a time when you felt most alive and purposeful. What were you doing? Who were you with? How can you recreate or integrate this feeling into your daily life?

Visualization: Close your eyes and visualize yourself reaching your full potential in the identified area. Picture the steps you need to take and the impact it will have on your life and others.

As you begin to uncover the depths of your potential, remember that this journey is just starting. With a clearer understanding of the wealth within, you're ready to set your sights on specific goals and targets, guiding you toward the life you've always dreamed of. In the next chapter, we'll explore how to clearly define these goals and set a course for success.

2
YOU CAN'T HIT A TARGET YOU DON'T HAVE

"Setting goals is the first step in turning the invisible into the visible." – Tony Robbins

In the tapestry of our lives, dreams are the initial threads woven with divine purpose. They are whispers of possibility, the faint echoes of what could be. Goals start with dreams. What are your dreams? Can you visualize them and verbalize them? To fuel the journey from potential to purpose, your dreams must ignite a burning desire within you, driving you toward the fulfillment of your divine destiny. Your dreams are important, and they are an excellent starting point as we continue on this journey from potential to purpose. However, a dream is in your head, and unfortunately, that's where it stays. In order to make it a reality, it has to take some sort of form.

A Target You Can See

PENTATHLON

Goal setting provides focus. It shapes your dreams. It gives you the ability to hone in on the exact actions you need to take to achieve everything you desire in life. It is the destination you are moving towards. In this way, a goal is a dream with a target.

I will never forget this story, Zig Ziglar shared. I was driving and listening to one of his sessions and what he shared changed my life. He talked about a famous archer, Howard Hill, and how he won every single one of the 267 archery contests he entered. He was like a real-life Robin Hood. He could hit a perfect bulls-eye at 50 feet, then split that first arrow with a second. It was almost too unbelievable to be seen. He had to retire prematurely because he kept winning every competition and there wasn't anyone who could compete with him. Zig Ziglar went on to ask a question that made me think.

Would it be possible for me to shoot better than Howard Hill?

What he said next, however, really got me thinking. But what followed was a bit confusing. He claimed that, with a blindfold on and spun around three times so he wouldn't know where the target was, I could hit bullseyes better than Howard Hill could on his best day.

Now I am sitting there in my car confused, but his next words changed everything for me. What he said next marked the beginning of my clarity. He said we would only have a greater chance at shooting better than Howard Hill because a man can't hit a target you can't see. Those beautiful words were followed by this question

"How can you hit a target you don't have?"

He literally, in that moment gave me the wisest counsel I had ever received. He showed me that all I had to do was enter my destination into the GPS. I knew where I wanted to go, but never wrote it down. And because I didn't write it down, I had no direction, no clarity, no course to follow.

Once I discovered what my dreams were, I was able to transform them into goals and targets that I could see.

How did I do that – and how can you do that? You write down your goals. Yes, this sounds too simple to work effectively, but it's true. Writing out your goal gives you the end to aim for, and then you can work backwards to develop the plan to get there. When your ideas and notes are written down as a goal, then it turns into something to pursue as a purpose.

"The trouble with not having a goal is that you can spend your life running up and down the field and never score." – Bill Copeland.

Specificity In Goals

Why isn't it good enough just to say, "I want a better job" or "I want more money." I thought, what's wrong with just wanting more money? Of course, there was nothing wrong with it except there is no real definition – could I see "more money" – how much more and for what?

Your goal should be clear and specific, otherwise, it's going to be hard to focus on actually accomplishing it. A good way to make sure your goal is specific is to answer the five "W" questions:

- What do I want to accomplish?
- Why is this important?
- Who is involved?
- Where is it located?
- Which resources or limitations are involved?

Measurable Goals

If you can't measure it, you can't manage it. As you pursue your dream, goal, and purpose, there should be small measurements built into the goal. Where there is measurable progress, you will notice when change occurs. How will you see when you're getting closer to your goal? It's a quantifying factor you built in.

A measurable goal should address questions such as:

- How much?
- How many?

Establish concrete criteria for measuring progress toward the attainment of each goal you set. When you measure your progress, you stay focused, meet your deadlines, and feel the excitement of getting closer to achieving your goal.

If you can't measure it, you can't manage it

Time-Bound Goals

It is important to associate a timeline with your goal. This moves it from the thought process of 'I will get around to it someday' to something that you have a clear idea of when you get to it or when you will ultimately complete it. If you do not set "achievement dates" for your goals, you'll get caught in the trap of "someday." As in, "Someday, I'll do that." If you were to open your calendar you will find: Sunday, Monday, Tuesday, Wednesday, Thursday, Friday, and Saturday. What you will not find is Someday. Someday will never come and all you're setting yourself up for is a journey of hope rather than purpose. You will just be waiting for someday to come, but I have news for you, it doesn't exist!

There are several factors to keep in mind when coming up with a timeline for your goal:

- Your goal should include a specific time by which you want to achieve it.

- When choosing a date by which you want to achieve your goal you need to be realistic.

- A timeline should be short enough to keep the goal challenging but long enough to keep it achievable.

Ownership Of Goals

In John Maxwell's book, "Putting Your Dream to The Test" he asked 10 questions that allows you to test your dream. The first question spoke volumes to me. It was the Ownership Question: Is my dream really my dream?

"Whatever you think, be sure it is what you think; whatever you want, be sure that it is what you want; whatever you feel, be sure that it is what you feel." — T. S. Eliot

I know what it is like to live someone else's dream. I tried to live my parents dream my whole life. And it wasn't that I was actually trying to live their dream, but rather I thought it was my dream. Both my dad and stepmom were interior designers and they had this dream of their children taking over the family business. I even went to Vo-Tech school to learn carpentry. We had it all planned out or rather they had it planned out.

You have to make sure your dream is actually your dream, otherwise, you will be living a life of untapped potential and fulfillment. You sacrifice who you were created to be. How tragic would it be to become successful in an area you were never meant to function in?

Accountability In Goals

If you set your goal and nobody knows about it, how much power does it have? Do you think it would make it easier to forget or start making excuses? To lose motivation? Without anyone holding you accountable to your goals, then you're not as likely to pursue them. A goal isn't as powerful if you don't have one or more people who can hold you accountable for it. Goals gain power when shared with trusted allies. Partnering with someone who understands and supports your vision can significantly enhance your chances of success.

A friend of mine, Hassan Johnson, was in the military with me. We both knew about goals, but we still had a problem with actually achieving them. We had joined a company together, and we had the ultimate end goal to make it to the top. We wrote down our goal and went at it, however, we didn't go really far. I lost motivation and I don't know what happened to him. But then I asked Hassan to be my workout partner. I wanted him to hold me accountable by calling me every other day to make sure I was still on course. By being that voice when I lost motivation to keep me going. I also did the same for him. Well, we not only reached our goals, but we ended up growing pretty large organizations. After he'd moved away to Miami, he and I were talking on the phone one day, and he actually confessed to me that it was easier to reach his goals when I was with him, and that having a partner helped him stay on track.

Going at it alone can almost guarantee failure, while having a support system is so powerful. The key is getting someone you trust and not getting offended when they keep it real. You need someone to be real with you. Sometimes, they've just got to tell it like it is. They will keep you on track and provide more support and help in reaching your goals.

"Your goals are the road maps that guide you and show you what is possible for your life."

- Les Brown

I mentioned earlier that you cannot hit a target you can't see or worst, don't have. If you don't write out and see your goals, you're likely not going to do anything about them. You could spend days, months, or even years just living your life, but not spending time pursuing your purpose. The graveyard is getting closer, so don't waste the time you have. In Iraq, I was given a second chance at life. I learned in that split second just how precious life is. This could be your second chance to take action and start the journey of turning your potential into purpose.

CHAPTER TWO

You Can't Hit a Target You Don't Have

> *"A goal without a plan is just a wish."*
>
> -Antoine de Saint-Exupéry

Summary

How have clear goals helped you in the past?

As we discussed in this chapter, it's hard to hit a target that you can't see. Setting clear, specific goals is crucial for achieving your dreams. This chapter emphasizes the importance of having a target to aim for and provides practical advice on goal-setting.

Reflection

Reflect on the importance of setting specific goals in your life. How have clear goals helped you in the past? Think about areas in your life where you could benefit from setting more specific goals.

Actionable Steps:

It's time to take action!

1. **Define Your Goals:** Transform your dreams into specific, measurable goals. Write down at least three concrete goals.

2. **Set Milestones:** Break down each goal into smaller milestones and set deadlines for each.

3. **Use SMART Criteria:** Ensure your goals are specific, measurable, achievable, relevant, and time-bound.

4. **Create a Vision Board:** Visualize your goals using a vision board, including images and words that represent your targets.

5. **Visualize Success:** Spend a few minutes each day visualizing the successful achievement of your goals.

Guided Exercise:

Goal Setting Worksheet: Use a worksheet to list your top three goals. For each goal, define the steps needed to achieve it, potential obstacles, and strategies to overcome them. Review and adjust your goals regularly.

Accountability Partner: Identify a friend or mentor to share your goals with. Schedule regular check-ins to discuss progress and challenges.

With clearly defined goals and a vision to guide you, you're equipped to navigate your journey with purpose. The next chapter will challenge you to shift your mindset, embracing growth and resilience as you face the inevitable obstacles along your path.

3

A Mindset Shift

"You must take personal responsibility. You cannot change the circumstances, the seasons, or the wind, but you can change yourself. That is something you have charge of." – Jim Rohn

As you're setting your goals and writing them down, you need to take the time to reflect on the person you need to become in order to achieve those goals. What steps do you need to take to ultimately become the person you need to become to achieve the goal?

The most significant benefit of setting goals isn't merely the achievement, but the transformation you undergo in the process. It's about the growth, the stretching of your capacities, and the refinement of your character.

Goals are a part of the entire journey from potential to purpose because they cause you to stretch and grow in ways that you never have before. In order to reach your goal, in order to maximize your potential, you must become better. And in becoming a better you, you will begin to move closer to your purpose.

Back in August 2011, my friend Hassan and I attended a leadership convention held at a Washington D.C. hotel. It was the first event we ever went to, and we were actually invited to go. While I was there, I met a very wealthy man. So, I asked him how did he get to where he is in life. I had dreams, goals, and aspirations. I needed to know! I asked him "What do I need to do to get to where you are?" His response was interesting. He said, "You're asking the wrong question." "The question isn't what do you need to do, but rather who do you need to become?" I stood there and as I was just pondering on what was just said, he spoke again, "Success isn't something you achieve, it's something you become."

As he said that, I thought about my life. I wasn't a good speaker, my oldest daughter was just born and I was working long hours in the military. I really didn't have any time to get better. How can someone like me become successful? All of a sudden, I went from a determined, passionate, motivated man, ready to learn and take control of my life, to a boy who was consumed with fear and excuses. It would be easier to achieve success if my life was different, I thought to myself. So, I told him, "It's easier to become when you have help." I was all alone on this journey. I mean I had my friend Hassan, but we were in the same boat. All I could think about was how we, how I, needed a mentor to achieve this kind of success. Someone who was further along the journey. Someone who had accomplished what I was looking to accomplish. And when you think about it, well that's true, but his response shocked me. He said, "Don't wish your life was easier, wish you were better." Then, what he said next, I have never forgotten and will never forget. "If you want to be a failure," he continued, "any excuse will work."

What's Your Excuse?

From that moment, all of my excuses went out the door. The excuses about not having time and mentors to help me. They were all gone. At the moment when this wealthy and successful man gave me his wise advice, I knew that successful people don't make excuses. They make things happen. So, I started focusing on becoming a better version of me.

When I attended that conference back in 2011, I was at a place in my life where excuses dominated my thinking. Honestly, I didn't know any better. All I'd known was hard times. That was my mindset because that was my reality. I also didn't know how much they were holding me back. I just thought there was no chance for me to be successful.

Excuses are rationalizations we make to ourselves about people, circumstances, and other things. They are invented reasons we create to defend ourselves. It's an internal problem, however we instead place the blame on external conditions. That internal problem is YOU! And what I mean by you is that you have to become, you have to grow, you have to get better. The more you grow, the less excuses you will have. Bottom line is you have to change.

In the military, they promoted professional development – which was important for the military to accomplish its mission. It's important in any career I'd imagine, but throughout my nine years in the Air Force, this was a huge deal. Professional development meant you cared about the mission and the mission was everything. But, what I actually found out was that if you develop yourself, you will be more effective professionally. The harder I worked on myself, the more value I added to myself.

For example, professional development says: Knowledge is Power. So those folks try to get you to learn as much as possible, in order for you to be effective at your job. Likewise, people go to school to learn and receive more professional development. But this means nothing without personal development. Personal development says: Knowledge is not power, but rather becomes powerful only when you apply it.

Author Charles Spurgeon once wrote, "Wisdom is the right use of knowledge." To just simply know is not to be wise. Many men know a great deal, and they are all the greater fools for it. There is no fool so great a fool as a knowing fool. But to know how to use knowledge is to have wisdom.

Personal development starts by taking 100 percent responsibility for everything in your life. This includes the level of your achievements, the results you produce or lack thereof, the quality of your relationships, the state of your health, your income, your debts, your feelings, your thoughts, and your emotions, too. Why? Because most of us have been conditioned to blame something outside of ourselves for the parts of our lives that we don't like or aren't working. For instance, do you blame any of the following people or situations for the setbacks in your life or for not having achieved everything you could've? This list includes your parents, bosses, spouse, friends, media, children, lack of money, lack of education, the president, and others.

These excuses and rationalizations stand in the way of your journey from potential to purpose. They are literally the lid to your potential and you are the only person that can remove the lid.

A Mindset Shift

Before I received this helpful advice about becoming, I was trying to figure out what I needed to do to unlock my potential and ultimately reach my purpose. Never did I think about who I needed to become. This changed everything. Most people, as they're pursuing their dreams or purpose, ask me what they need to do to reach it. But, they're asking the wrong question. You should be asking: Who do I have to become to reach it?

Once I learned this life-changing secret, I started to shift my focus from what I was doing to who I was becoming. I wanted to be the best version of myself I could be.

Becoming is potential being manifested.

That wealthy man at the leadership conference taught me that I couldn't achieve my goals without becoming a better person. My goals were challenging and hard to reach. And I couldn't achieve them when I first began, way back at the starting line. I had just started to understand how important it was to activate and unlock my potential. But the more I grew, my potential started to manifest.

You have to become in order to achieve.

Kevin Bracy said, "If you want your life to be different, you have to be willing to do something different first." Which means if you want something to change, you have to change. You have to change and become what you are pursuing. If you don't, you will continue living with your potential that hasn't been activated yet.

Who Must You Become?

In the chapter on goals, I talked about knowing the end first, so that you know what target you're aiming at. I knew what my purpose was, so then I had to figure out who must I become to ultimately achieve it. I set the goal to be a speaker and speak all over the world, so I asked myself: Who must I become to ultimately reach this purpose?

- I knew I had to become great at speaking, so I started to practice. I listened and watched other great speakers.
- I knew I needed to develop a better vocabulary, so I started to read.
- I know that speaking involves selling your story, so I learned sales.
- I knew that I had the tendency to procrastinate, and that I would never be a great speaker if I didn't become proactive.

- I knew that speaking involved connecting with people, so I worked on being approachable. I also became more outgoing, so I could see how people feel, think, etc.

After I'd listed the things I needed to do, I started reading books. You change your thinking; you change your life. I read books written by the mentors that I wanted to follow. I also started working on my beliefs about myself. I would look in the mirror and speak things aloud over and over about myself. Things like:

- "I am confident."
- "I will do great things."
- "I will be the best me."

This may sound weird or funny! But, it works. I swear it. Something small but powerful started to happen to me. My perspective started to shift. My perspective changed from what I wasn't capable of – to what I could learn to add value to who I am. Everything became a school.

You grow to be great by learning. Look at every situation as a school, and you will always learn. How can this person teach you or show you what you need to become?

When I would go to work, I remember my boss who always had a smile on his face. He had a great outlook on life and it seemed like nothing really bothered him. To be honest, this bothered me. Why was this guy always happy? He was the only guy I knew, that looked forward to Mondays. What was it? At first, I thought it was fake, but it seemed real. One time I was so curious that I approached him and said, "It seems like nothing bothers you." "Why are you so happy? It's Monday!" He said, "Don't ever try to just get through the day. Rather, get from the day."

Talk about perspective

He taught me that day to treat every day like a school. I learned that day, that life was just a journey of untapped knowledge. That the greatest library in the world wasn't in a building, the top school wasn't some prestige university, but that the greatest wealth of knowledge is right in front of us. It's this thing called life and if we stop trying to just get through the day but get from the day, we would grow every day.

You have to focus on becoming, and the more you become, the closer you will get to your goal.

Are you becoming the person you need to become to achieve your goal?

The Heart of the Journey

This concept can work for any goal that you set. If a person is trying to lose weight, what type of person must they become? You need to examine yourself and be honest. Ask yourself questions about who you need to become. “Am I lazy?” Then, work on that. “Do I eat out a lot?” Then, work on that. You have to become what you’re trying to become.

Don’t focus on the goal. So many people focus on the thing they want to have (thin body, more money, etc.), rather than asking themselves who they need to be in order to then achieve those goals.

A lot of goal-setting material doesn't focus on this aspect of 'becoming,' either. They just advise readers to 'set goals and work towards them.' But that doesn't work if your goal requires you to change, and you're not prepared to do that.

We should really be growth-oriented, rather than goal-oriented. Goals focus on the destination, while growth focuses on the journey. Growth encompasses you working on yourself and becoming better. Your goal is the destination. The pursuit is the road you take to get there. This is the heart of the journey from potential to purpose.

"It's not the blowing of the wind that determines your destination. It's the set of the sail."
- Jim Rohn

Jim Rohn said that it's not the wind that determines our destination but the set of our sail. He was right. I no longer dwell on the excuses and reasons I had for not pursuing my purpose. Instead, I focus on setting a better sail to reach my purpose and fully maximize my potential. And you set a better sail by becoming the person you need to become, to ultimately achieve your goal.

CHAPTER THREE

A Mindset Shift

> *"You cannot change the circumstances, the seasons, or the wind, but you can change yourself."*
> -Jim John

Summary

Are there any limiting beliefs holding you back?

This chapter discusses how to achieve success, emphasizing that it's not so much about what you have to do, but about who you need to become. What excuses do you need to stop making? What steps do you need to start taking to become better? Here are some questions for you to think about:

Reflection

Reflect on your current mindset. Are there any limiting beliefs holding you back? Consider how a growth mindset can help you achieve your goals.

1. What are my excuses for not achieving success?

2. Where do these excuses come from?

3. What do I need to ensure that these excuses no longer become my reality?

4. What can I do daily to counteract these excuses that fear creates?

Actionable Steps:

It's time to take action!

1. **Positive Affirmations:** Write and repeat daily affirmations that reinforce your belief in your potential.
2. **Mindfulness Practice:** Spend 5-10 minutes each day practicing mindfulness or meditation to stay present and focused.
3. **Seek Feedback:** Ask a trusted friend or mentor for feedback on your mindset and areas for improvement.
4. **Mindset Journaling:** Each night, journal about any negative thoughts you had during the day and reframe them positively.
5. **Growth Mindset Activities:** Engage in activities that challenge you and help you grow, such as learning a new skill or taking on a new project.

Guided Exercise:

Affirmation Practice: Write down three limiting beliefs you currently hold. For each, create a positive affirmation that counteracts it. Repeat these affirmations daily, ideally in front of a mirror.

Mindset Reflection: Reflect on a recent challenge and identify how a growth mindset could have altered your approach. Write down the lessons learned and how you can apply a growth mindset in future situations.

Embracing a growth mindset is crucial for transforming potential into reality. As you shed limiting beliefs and adopt a resilient attitude, you're better prepared to face life's challenges. Next, we delve into understanding the role of our circumstances and how to redefine our identity, ensuring that we are not confined by the hand we've been dealt.

4

Just The Hand I Was Dealt

"The greater part of our happiness or misery depends on our dispositions and not our circumstances." – Martha Washington

Picture this. You're sitting at a card table, looking at a bad hand of cards. The card dealer gave you those low-number cards, and in a game like that, there's nothing you can do about it. You can't say, "Hey, dealer, I'd like Kings, Queens, and Aces."

Is your life filled with low numbers, like that game? Do you feel you were dealt a bad hand in life? That you have bad circumstances around you? Your family could have struggled with money, so you grew up poor. You didn't have the option of pursuing your potential, because you were just trying to help put food on the table. Maybe you had to grow up too fast. The days of imagining a dream that got you excited were cut short.

"Your present circumstances don't determine where you can go; they merely determine where you start." – Nido Qubein

It's easy to let the circumstances around you dictate your potential, keeping you from activating it and discovering your own buried treasure. I let mine dictate my life for many years because I didn't know any different. I grew up living in a car, in a warehouse, in a storage unit, and in and out of shelters. I wasn't sure from one month to the next what roof would be over my head. I didn't even know what kind of bed would be beneath me as I lay down to sleep each night. It changed all the time. Many times, there was no bed at all. I had muscles I didn't even know existed before, because they would ache from the uncomfortable places I was forced to sleep.

I remember my dad sneaking us out of this store we slept at to take us to school every morning. If you looked at this kid sleeping in a store, you would think he'd be the last person to have any potential or dreams come true. When I was homeless, all I knew was that lifestyle. I never thought I could have more or be more. My potential was literally stagnant because of who I thought I was.

These challenges and obstacles that created my circumstances at the time did limit my potential, because they created an identity. And then we take the identity that the world has labeled us and try to do the best we can in this thing called life. However, we can't let challenges mold us or control us. If we did, then we would never fully reach our purpose.

Your identity will dictate your destiny

To effectively answer the question "Why am I here?" we must first answer "Who am I?" The "who" affects the "why." We all seek to understand why we were created, to unlock our potential, and to live a life full of purpose. But we will never experience the "why" if we don't discover the "who." Your identity will dictate your destiny.

Identity is an accumulation of beliefs you have about who you are as a person. It is how you see yourself. Your self-identity is not who you are, but who you think you are. Our belief becomes our conduct. We behave according to our beliefs. In fact, it is not possible to live in a way that violates what we believe about ourselves. A person who is convinced that he is abandoned will live as an abandoned person. A girl who thinks she doesn't measure up will operate out of her distorted view.

You are not what you think you are, but rather what you believe you are.

Now belief is a word that we are all familiar with, however, I don't think many of us are familiar with what it really means. Why? Because many of us confuse the word belief with the word thought. There is a difference between your thoughts and your beliefs. A thought is resident in your mind. A belief is resident in your heart. Beliefs are often connected to repeated experiences that seem true because they occur so frequently. They are often connected to traumatic experiences from our lives, and over time, we become convinced of their truth. These beliefs become the lens through which we view reality and, eventually, shape our reality.

Examples include:

- I'm ugly.
- I will always be rejected.
- I'm not good enough.

- I'm not smart enough.

See, it is not what's in your mind that determines your experiences, but rather what is in your heart. And these beliefs can be so far hidden in your heart, that they will limit you from maximizing your potential. These beliefs can become your identity, limiting you from fulfilling your purpose.

A belief is not just in your heart but rather over your heart, like a contact lens being placed over your heart through which you perceive your experiences. I remember a Pastor, Bob Hamp, sharing a story of a little girl who had a communication barrier with her father at a young age. Every time she would try to talk to her dad, he would disconnect. He would unintentionally push her away. It was almost as if her dad was giving her this stiff arm. So what happened was she developed this contact lens over her heart that said "Men will always reject me." Now, every time she approached a male, she had this expectation of being rejected from a belief that formed.

We have to take the lens of our experiences off and put on a new set of lenses. Because your identity will dictate your future. Your identity will dictate your destiny. How you see yourself is how you will be.

A New Lens

You have to start to declare what you want. You have to speak over your life what you want to see and become.

> *"Whether you think you can, or you think you can't, you are right."* – Henry Ford

What we say about ourselves, we tend to believe. What we believe, we tend to act. What we act, we tend to become. Charles Schwab said, "When a man puts a limit on what he will do, he places a limit on what he can do." How you view yourself and what you speak out of your mouth will be your ceiling. You are the lid to your potential.

We all have potential, but it's tied to how we see and view ourselves. This is one of the many enemies we will face as we go on this journey from potential to purpose. Let's take a look at some of the others we are up against.

CHAPTER FOUR Just the Hand I was Dealt

> *The greater part of our happiness or misery depends on our dispositions and not our circumstances"*
>
> -Martha Washington

Summary

How can you reframe your story to focus on your strengths?

So, what was "the hand that you were dealt" that has shaped your reality? How do you see yourself? How do you see the world around you? What has hindered you? What has helped you? By realizing that the hand that you were dealt plays into your purpose on this earth, it should be appreciated and not eulogized. For some, you will never have a passion for helping the homeless, if you never knew what it felt like to be homeless. You will never be able to help those who have been rejected if you've never experienced rejection. The hand you were dealt is a combination of other people's choices, demographics, etc, but ultimately it was the choice that God used for your life because out of it could come great things.

Reflection

Reflect on how your upbringing and circumstances have influenced your identity. Consider how you can reframe your story to focus on your strengths and potential.

Actionable Steps:

It's time to take action!

1. **Reframe Your Story:** Write a new narrative for yourself that focuses on your strengths and potential.
2. **Create Identity Statements:** Develop statements that reflect who you are becoming, such as "I am resilient" or "I am resourceful."
3. **Gratitude Practice:** Start a daily gratitude journal to acknowledge positive aspects of your life and progress.
4. **Visualize Your Future Self:** Spend time each day visualizing yourself as the person you want to become.
5. **Affirm Your Identity:** Throughout the day, repeat your identity statements to reinforce your new self-concept.

Guided Exercise:

Life Assessment Grid: Create a grid assessing different areas of your life (e.g., career, relationships, health). Rate your satisfaction in each area from 1-10. Identify areas for growth and potential actions.

Identity Exploration: Write a letter to your future self, describing the person you want to become. Include specific qualities, achievements, and the steps you took to get there.

As you redefine your identity and set new standards, you empower yourself to rise above your circumstances. The journey forward will require confronting fears that may hold you back. In the next chapter, we will explore how to face these fears head-on and move confidently toward our goals.

5
Facing My Enemy

"I've learned that fear limits you and your vision. It serves as blinders to what may be just a few steps down the road for you. The journey is valuable, but believing in your talents, your abilities, and your self-worth can empower you to walk down an even brighter path. Transforming fear into freedom - how great is that?" – Soledad O'Brien

I faced a huge enemy in Iraq, and it was easy to see that enemy and work alongside my fellow soldiers to defeat that enemy. When you can stand on a battlefield and there's the enemy right across from you, it's clear who you're fighting against.

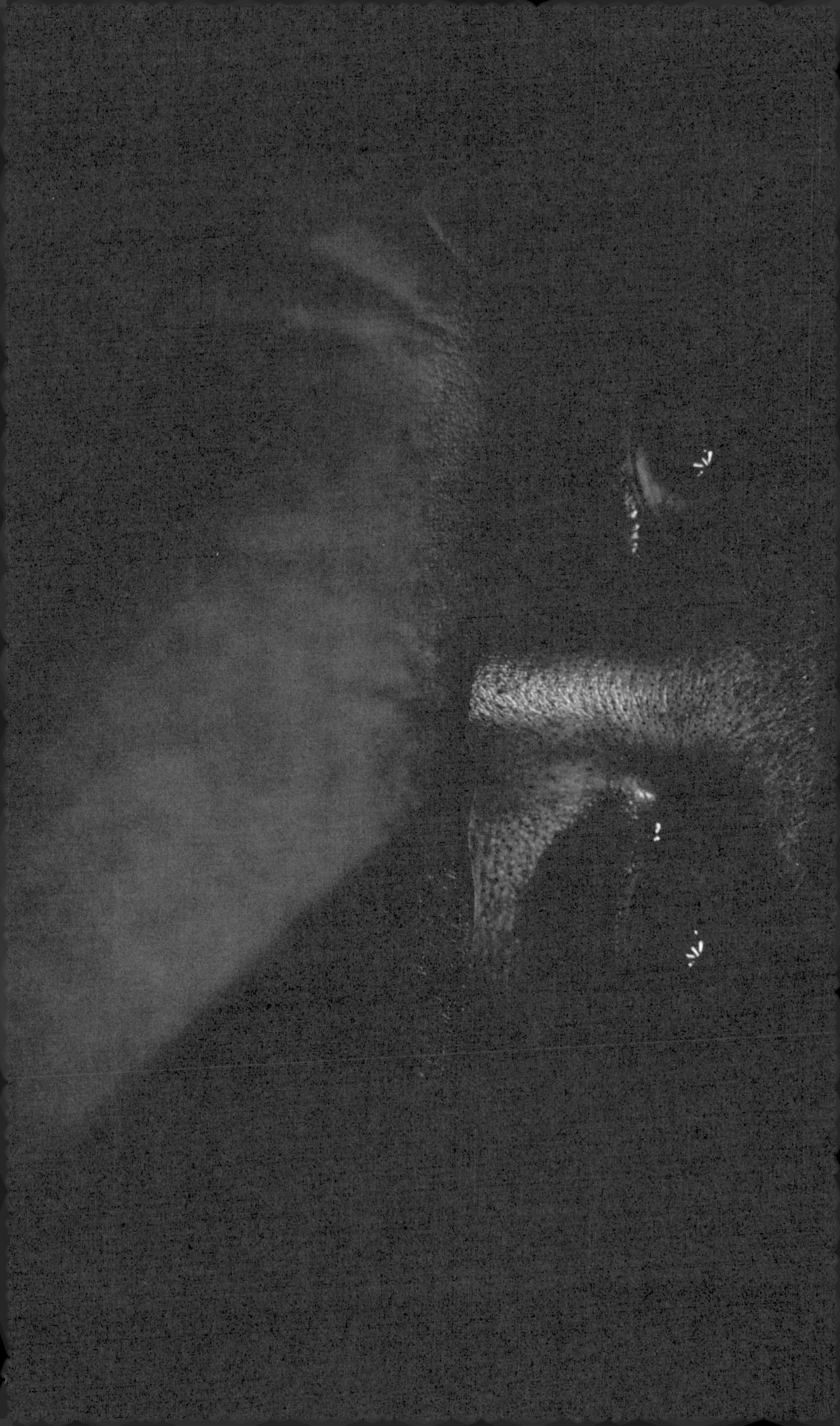

Not every enemy is there in plain sight. Some of the most powerful enemies you will ever face in your life are invisible. But, make no mistake, they are powerful and they will stop you from activating your potential and uncovering your personal buried treasure.

Fear can be one of the hardest enemies you will ever face.

You have dreams for your life, yet it can sometimes feel impossible to make them real. You might know what to do and even how to do it, but taking action requires courage — the ability to withstand fear, humiliation, and discomfort. We are conditioned from childhood to avoid unpleasant feelings. Nothing stirs those feelings more than taking risks, which is necessary to go after your dreams. It's no wonder change can feel so hard.

"Growth requires change and potential requires growth."

Change is a necessary part of life. When you think about it, if there was nothing changing, then there wouldn't be life as we know it. Our lives are actually fueled by change, though most of us want the comfort of stability.

"Life begins at the end of your comfort zone."
– Neale Donald Walsch

My first major encounter with change was one of the hardest decisions of my life. Serving in the military for nine years, I was used to change, but this one was a shock to me and an even more shock to my family. I reached a point where I decided to separate from the military, letting go of nine years of service and a very comfortable lifestyle for the sake of pursuing a dream. To make matters worse, the pursuit of my dream would require me to have to travel from DC to NJ which was an average of nine hours there and back. And this was twice a week! People thought I was crazy. My family thought I was making a mistake. I will never forget a conversation with my in-laws that almost caused me to give up on my dream. "Was I making a mistake?" I thought. I mean, I totally understand their concerns, I had a family, their family, that I was responsible for. And I was leaving security for, well, for a dream.

I separated from the military and went after it. I went after my dream! And just as things started to go well, another dream surfaced. A bigger dream! I will never forget that moment when my father-in-law came to visit us and he was sharing how proud he was of me. I followed my dream and it was going great. We had a beautiful home, making great money and my in-laws were happy. I finally got their approval and thought to myself, "I have to tell them that the dream has gotten bigger." I had to share with them that I was about to make another change that seemed even riskier than the first one. I was about to give up everything to pursue another dream, just when my in-laws finally accepted the first.

T. E. Lawrence said, "All men dream, but not equally. Those who dream by night in the dusty recesses of their minds, wake in the day to find that it was vanity: but the dreamers of the day are dangerous men, for they may act on their dreams with open eyes, to make them possible."

I had another, a bigger dream that was going to require me to give up even more than before. We were giving up multiple six-figures, and everything we had built to pursue this first dream.

The cycle started again. People thought I was crazy and my family didn't understand what we were doing. They asked, "Why are you going backwards?" But change had to happen for me to accomplish this dream. Sacrifice had to take place for me to ultimately pursue and reach my fullest potential.

When we begin to realize that change is not something to be feared and avoided, we can learn to let go of the fear of change. We can let go of the parts of us that have been refusing to change, often causing considerable stress in our lives. The only way to accept change is to realize that it is inevitable and that we can't keep it from happening. The world around us is expanding and growing by constant change. Why do we think we are different?

Don't let fear stop you from reaching your full potential.

Think of fear as the enemy in your mind that doesn't want to see you get hurt, so it keeps you safe. But keeping you safe isn't a bad thing, right? You wouldn't want to put yourself in dangerous situations all the time that might hurt or even kill you, especially if you have a family that relies on you. In that example, fear is a good thing. But that's where it can be deceiving. It doesn't just keep you safe, it keeps you stuck. You become too scared to take a chance to set goals, pursue your dreams, and find your purpose. Fear holds you back. Fear limits your potential.

Fear was a huge enemy of mine. It was something I had to overcome because of the many things that happened to me as a young man. It was actually one family member in particular who caused me to feel the most fear. When fear comes from your own family, that can be the biggest enemy of all to overcome. That's all you ever know, and it can be difficult, almost impossible to imagine a different way of living.

I felt scared a lot while growing up. It was my knee-jerk reaction to the things my dad did or said to me. I was scared to do things. I was scared to say things because my dad was tough. He wanted the best for his kids and because of that, he was really tough on us. This was my life growing up and I didn't know how to process it and fear consumed me.

The thing about fear is – it doesn't matter how it enters your life; it can and will affect so many other areas of your life. Thanks to the constant fear I lived with when I was growing up, I never had the courage to pursue any of my dreams. I never had the courage to do or say anything.

Perhaps you share some of the same fears I had. I was afraid of failure. I was afraid of what people thought and what they would think of me. I was afraid of letting down the people I loved and wanted to impress. I was afraid of not making people proud of me. I was just afraid. Fear took away my confidence in myself and my hopes for the future. Fear had put a cap on my potential. Fear didn't just limit me, it stopped me dead in my tracks.

Facing Your Fears

You dream of doing something great. You dream of unlocking the buried treasure of potential inside of you. So, how come you're not able to push yourself to do it? It's because of these limiting beliefs caused by fear. You need to remove these limiting beliefs and push past your fear. Well, how do you get started?

One simple way to start today is by using positive affirmations about yourself. Consistently using positive self-talk will boost your confidence level. Focus on the small victories that you've overcome in life, not the things that hold you back. Change your thinking from fear talk to victory talk.

There are more methods to overcoming fear. Here are a few that have worked for me:

- Therapy: Yes, it can be difficult to admit that you need some outside help, but it can be highly beneficial, even life-changing. It's worth it to find a good therapist. They can help you explore your background to identify the fears that are holding you back.

- Reading: There are many books available that address various fears, including fear of public speaking, fear of failure, fear of success, and every other kind of fear you can think of. Reading a good book about your specific fear can open new doors on how you can overcome it.

- Find a role model: Many famous and successful people faced a rocky road on their journey to unlocking their potential and living out their purpose. Find someone who had the fear you have, but managed to transcend it. Get in touch with them, ask how they did it, and see if it could work for you. They don't have to be well-known, either. Maybe a friend of yours has overcome a similar fear.

- Surround yourself with positive people: There's a saying that you are the average of the five people you most associate with. If they bring you down, then you will not be able to show the world your purpose. Join groups and find people who show you positive character traits such as confidence, outgoingness, courage, generosity, and any other positive traits. Be warned that as you evaluate your circle, some people may not make the cut. You have to take inventory of who you have around you most. They could be the cap to your future.

- Practice doing what you fear the most: One of my favorite quotes is by the great American writer Mark Twain, who wrote, "Do the thing you fear most and the death of fear is certain." If you want the fear inside you to die and stop limiting your potential, the best thing you can do is – yes, do what you fear the most. Whether you are afraid of public speaking or afraid of heights, the more you do it, the better you become at it. Then the better you get, the less fear you have.

- Faith: This is the number one way I have been able to overcome the many fears in my life. Overcoming fear doesn't get rid of fear. I have learned that fear is a constant battle that has to be won every single day. I heard John Maxwell say that when your faith outweighs your fear, you will move past the fear. Such a powerful and true statement. Your faith has to be stronger than the fear and once your faith increases, you can conquer anything.

An Enemy Defeated

I was in Dubrovnik on a missions trip with a friend of mine, Daryian Kelton. He was absolutely terrified of heights. Me and my other friends were having a blast jumping off this cliff into the water, but Daryian wouldn't do it. He was scared, he refused, and he was not going to do it...

Until, suddenly, he did. He jumped!

Do you know what happened to him? He not only had fun jumping in the water, but this one literal leap of faith caused a spiral effect in his life. Because, if he could do that, then perhaps he could overcome other fears. That's exactly what he did. He started to attack many of the other fears in his life, all because he confronted and defeated this one huge enemy.

Watching Daryian overcome his fear of heights that day had a powerful effect on me too. When we see people conquer and then beat what is holding them back, it inspires us as well. The world is full of enemies. But it's full of heroes, too. Heroes can be everyday people, just like you and me, who overcome this huge inner enemy of fear.

I hope you take these examples and stories to get you motivated about overcoming fear every day. Don't let your fear be the lid to your potential.

"It is not death that a man should fear, but he should fear never beginning to live."
– Marcus Aurelius

CHAPTER FIVE

Facing My Enemy

> *He who is afraid of a thing gives it power over him.*
>
> -Moorish Proverb

Summary

How have fear limited your potential and progress?

Some enemies are visible, while others are not. Often, the greatest enemies are the ones you can't see, as they tend to influence how you perceive everything else. Fear is one of the biggest enemies that everyone faces in so many different ways. There are many different types of fear. There is a fear of spiders as well as a fear of change. Fear is so powerful because it creates an awareness of something. A fear of swimming is attached to the understanding or the awareness of drowning, maybe because of a particular experience. Let's talk about some of your fears and why you believe they affect you. For example, fear of attending an interview often stems from the awareness that you might not be hired. But the alternative to that could be that you will get hired or even if you don't, there may be a better job for you. So, let's talk about your fears, the awareness that those fears bring, and then the alternative to counteract the fear.

Fear:________________________________

Awareness:____________________________

Alternative:___________________________

Reflection

Reflect on the fears that have held you back in the past. How have they limited your potential and progress? Consider moments when you faced your fears and overcame them. What did you learn from those experiences?

Actionable Steps:

It's time to take

1. **Identify Fears:** Write down your fears and the beliefs underlying them.

2. **Gradual Exposure:** Face your fears by gradually exposing yourself to them in less intimidating scenarios.

3. **Learn from Fear:** Reflect on past experiences where fear held you back and extract lessons from those moments.

4. **Build Resilience:** Engage in activities that challenge you to step outside your comfort zone regularly.

5. **Reward Yourself:** Celebrate your successes, no matter how small, each time you confront and overcome a fear.

Guided Exercise:

Fear Mapping: List your fears and rate them on a scale of 1-10 in terms of intensity. For each fear, write down one small step you can take to confront it.

Exposure Challenge: Choose one fear to focus on this week. Plan a specific activity that confronts this fear and reflect on the experience afterward.

Overcoming fear is a critical step in unlocking your full potential. By facing your fears and building resilience, you can break free from the limitations that hold you back. In the next chapter, we'll address the subtle yet powerful enemy of comparison, exploring how it can rob you of joy and hinder your progress.

6

The Death Of Joy

"The reason why we struggle with insecurity is because we compare our behind the scenes with everyone else's highlight reel." – Steven Furtick

While the enemy of fear is a strong one and can be hard to recognize, the enemy of comparison is much harder to see as the enemy that it really is. It's so simple and second nature to compare yourself to other people. But, this can also limit your potential.

I really loved music when I was a little kid. My siblings and I learned music and played together pretty much every day. My dad watched over our long rehearsals and didn't stop until we got it right. We weren't allowed to eat and we certainly weren't allowed to leave until it was perfect. People would joke and call him Joe Jackson.

As a kid, I grew up watching my dad play and wanted to be like him. Many of us look up to and idolize our parents. They seem like they are doing everything right and they are successful in our young eyes. I tried to emulate his music-playing style, I thought it would make him happy for me to sound like him. But that wasn't the case. Instead of being proud of me or encouraging me, my dad would get mad. He'd say to me, "You sound like me," as if it was a bad thing. It almost sounded like he was accusing me of something I wasn't. "Get your own sound," he'd tell me. I felt bad because that was kind of like being rejected by my dad.

At the time, I was young and didn't understand what he was saying. I also didn't get that there was a lesson in that. He was actually saying to not be the best HIM, but to be the best ME. It wasn't an easy lesson to learn, as all the great lessons are. He wanted me to be the best version of me. He didn't want me to sound like him, but he wanted me to be better than him. This was one of the best lessons my dad has ever taught me. However, at a young age, comparison was birthed. I just thought I wasn't good enough. I didn't understand what he was trying to teach me and from that, I began to compare myself to everyone.

> *"The only person you should try to be better than is who you were yesterday."* – Unknown

Comparing myself to my dad was the beginning of something toxic that could have contaminated me for the rest of my life if I hadn't overcome it. I generally find that comparison is the fast track to unhappiness. No one ever compares themselves to someone else and comes out even. Nine times out of ten, we compare ourselves to people who are somehow better than us and end up feeling more inadequate.

Comparison is like a disease of the mind. It actually comes from envy, since you are envious of somebody else's talents, accomplishments, achievements, or success rather than honoring, acknowledging, or celebrating your own. You need to look at yourself and what you're doing, rather than comparing yourself to others.

Many years after that incident with my dad, I was at my first duty station as a young Air Force Cadet, fresh out of boot camp. Even though I was at the beginning of my brand-new career, I felt like I really accomplished something. I was ready for this new chapter in my life. There I was at the time, in Florida, out of my parents' house, and ready to start a new life.

I wanted to continue doing the music that I loved as a kid, so I remember going to an audition for a singing group. I actually met my gorgeous wife Torri there, but that's another story! I would compare myself to her every day and fall short, but continued smiling every time I fell!

Anyway, I ended up getting picked up as one of this singing group's keyboard players. Sam Hill was their music director and also their lead keyboardist. He also quickly became the person I compared myself to basically every day. Everything he did was so much cooler and better than me. He was always wailing away on those black and white keys, playing riffs and chords and these awesome runs. Just top talent right there. I couldn't play like that. I couldn't make the keyboard sing like Sam could. It was like an extension of his fingers. There was magic in those hands!

Well, with talent like Sam Hill, I was always going to be second fiddle next to him. How could I not be? He was awesome, and I was mediocre. But what I soon realized was that by comparing myself to him, I was in his lane. Just as if I was in a car trying to take over his side of the road.

That's pretty dangerous! Because when driving this car, which is you, through the course of life, if you don't stay in your lane and concentrate on your own road, you are bound to crash – and crash hard. Which is exactly what happened to me. Instead of moving forward and becoming a better keyboard player, I started to crash. I knew the first signs of this were happening because I felt the envy. It was damaging my self-worth. "Comparison is the death of joy," as genius writer Mark Twain wrote. My joy with music in the group was certainly dying, because I was comparing myself too much to Sam Hill.

My life became consumed with what I wasn't, instead of what I could be. I wasn't looking at my own lawn, at my own garden. I thought that the grass was greener on that other lawn. And it was, but as long as I was focused on that other lawn, I wouldn't be able to work on my own lawn. My identity started to shift, and I began to become what I was thinking, inadequate and never good enough.

"Comparison is the death of joy." – Mark Twain"

Comparing yourself to others breeds feelings not only of envy, but low self-confidence, and, in many cases, even depression. When I was having these feelings and struggling with my identity, I was fighting the downward spiral of comparison. I'd compare myself to others, fall short, feel worse, look at them again, feel even worse, and so on. It just pulled me downward. There was nowhere else to go. Fear may block you from moving forward, but comparison is like drowning. You just keep going down.

I thought I was worthless. As I kept having those feelings of worthlessness, it got even worse. I was becoming what I thought about. My identity changed, and I certainly wasn't activating my potential. Instead, I just felt like I had no energy or desire to move forward with my goals and my life purpose. I just felt kind of dead inside.

Take care not to compare yourself to others. It is consuming, in more ways than one. It consumes your self-worth, it consumes your identity, and it also consumes your time. Every day that you spend comparing yourself to others and coming up short is one more lost day that you could have spent pursuing your life purpose.

When you focus on other people's strengths – or what you believe to be their strengths – then you shift the focus off finding your own strength. You can't hear your own voice when you're listening to somebody else's voice all the time. It drowns you out. You've got to work on yourself, not compare yourself to others. Once you move the focus to yourself and your own goals, that's when you start to heal this disease of the mind.

Just imagine the difference it would make if you re-channeled all the energy you spend on comparing to developing yourself. You become your ultimate frame of reference, tracking yourself against yourself. Are you fitter than you used to be? Are you making progress toward your goals?

We all have our own hurdles to scale, fears to conquer, and paths to forge. So run your own race and let others run theirs. Other people have their own potential, their own goals, and their own life purposes. A doctor doesn't compare himself to a painter and wish he could have created art, when his real purpose is to save lives.

If he did, then he'd be consumed with comparison – and he might waste so much time, he'd become part of the riches in the cemetery. It's sad when he could have been the doctor he was always supposed to be and made a difference in living his purpose.

Your potential is important. Your dreams are important. Your goals are important. Your life purpose is important.

Now, it's time to pursue what you are here to do.

CHAPTER SIX

The Death of Joy

The only person you should try to be better than is who you were yesterday"

-Unkown

Summary

How has comparison impacted your ability to pursue your goals?

Comparison kills joy. If we all looked the same and did the same things, the world would be a boring place. Even if someone is going after a purpose, or has a gift that is similar to yours, you bring a special uniqueness to it, which makes it altogether different. In society, we are faced with comparisons all the time, which cause people to not pursue their dreams, or not be confident in themselves because they're making other people their standard. The unique purpose and gifts that were given to you should be the standard. The closer you are to bringing that purpose into fulfillment is the standard by which you should compare yourself to.

Reflection

Reflect on how comparison has affected your self-worth and joy. How has it impacted your ability to pursue your goals? Consider the areas of your life where you often compare yourself to others. How can you shift your focus back to your own growth?

1. Do you compare yourself to others when it comes to your gifts and purpose?

2. What causes you to doubt what you have to offer?

3. What makes you stand out from everyone else?

4. What can help you overcome the killer of joy which is comparison?

Actionable Steps:

It's time to take

1. **Self-Comparison:** Set personal benchmarks to compare your progress against your past self.

2. **Limit Social Media:** Reduce exposure to social media or other platforms that trigger comparison.

3. **Celebrate Wins:** Celebrate your achievements, no matter how small, to build confidence and joy.

4. **Daily Reflection:** Spend 5 minutes each evening reflecting on your own progress and growth.

5. **Positive Influences:** Surround yourself with people who inspire and support your journey.

Guided Exercise:

Gratitude Journal: Start a gratitude journal, noting down three things you are grateful for each day, focusing on personal achievements and qualities.

Comparison Detox: Spend a week actively avoiding comparisons. If you find yourself comparing, redirect your thoughts to something positive about your own journey.

Letting go of comparison frees you to fully embrace your unique path and potential. As you focus on your own journey, the importance of understanding your underlying motivations becomes clear. In the next chapter, we'll explore the power of discovering your 'why' and how it can propel you toward your goals.

7
The Power Of Why

"When you feel like quitting think about why you started." – Anonymous

Once you realize you have this buried treasure of potential inside you waiting to be activated, you have the target you're aiming for, and your course is set with your sails in the right direction – then it's time to really put the motivation in place for you to continue on your journey from potential to purpose.

I have to be honest with you, the road is tough. We've talked about overcoming fear, comparing yourself to others, and the excuses and reasons that will block your path, but it's easier to talk about enemies than it is to fight them. And you will fight them every day as you grow and change. Growth is hard. It requires a strong character and a strong commitment to your purpose.

WHY?

John C Maxwell said it best when he said, "Every journey toward a dream is personal, and as a result, so is the price that must be paid to achieve it." He went on to say:

- "The journey will take longer than you hoped.
- "The obstacles will be more numerous than you believed."
- "The disappointments will be greater than you expected."
- "The lows will be lower than you imagined."
- "The price will be higher than you anticipated."

This is the reality that many people are just not ready and prepared for. This journey is not easy. It wasn't easy for me! So what keeps you going?

What keeps you getting up every day when you don't feel like it? What keeps you from giving up when it gets hard? Because it's going to get hard.

Your Why!

Without a strong 'why' and a strong motivation in place, there's a big chance that you'll give up. You will likely fail and quit. And it won't be because you're a weak person or your goals aren't great or you don't deserve it. You'll want to give up because growth is hard. It stretches you and takes you out of your comfort zone. That's, well, uncomfortable! And you won't have anything that will pull you past it.

"Your goal will push you but your why will pull you."

I don't want you to quit and give up. Motivation is like a continuous energy hit. It pumps you up and fuels you more to tackle the next obstacle. You've got to have your 'why' – and it's got to be so strong that it reminds you every day why you're doing what you're doing and pulls you past any challenge that will confront you. Your 'why' can't be something normal or mundane. Many people will see a picture of an expensive luxury lifestyle and immediately say, "I want that!" They want those clothes, that house, that car, and all those expensive things. But just saying, "I want that" isn't enough for you to actually get the motivation to go after those things. Your 'want' has to go deeper – so that you take action to get what you want.

"It does not matter how slowly you go as long as you do not stop." - Confucius

Motivation is like brushing your teeth. You need to do it every day. Just the same, you need to motivate yourself every day because it will wear off. It wears off quickly because stuff will happen in your life. People will say discouraging things to you. An unexpected bill arrives in the mail. Your daughter is unexpectedly sick on the day you were planning on doing something big towards your purpose. Setbacks will happen all the time.

What will keep you going when you have more months at the end of the money? Or when you get tired? Or when people keep saying no? What will keep you going when your family doesn't support you? Or when doors slam in your face or you just fail time after time? What's going to keep you motivated?

It's your WHY. It has to be so strong that you will go through a brick wall to reach your destination. It's the strength inside you that keeps you going. Everybody faces failure. Every single person overcomes obstacles and has brick walls to face.

Challenges and obstacles are going to come. If your WHY isn't strong in your core, then you will succumb to the failure and quit. But, if you're able to get past setbacks and failures, holding on to your WHY, and still staying on target to reach your goal, you'll discover the same thing that I did:

The hardest obstacles bring the sweetest reward.

You appreciate the success simply because you worked so hard for it. You were tested and you passed. When you reach small targets on your way to your bigger goals, you may even cry, you're so happy and you fought so hard for it. You'll feel on top of the world. You'll feel like you won a gold medal! You will function in purpose.

The most rewarding job I ever had was by far the hardest training I've ever been in. I'd joined the

Air Force Honor Guard, which is a prestigious Presidential Unit. The training was like boot camp times one hundred. My hours consisted of waking up at three o'clock in the morning to be at work by four in the morning. Then, I'd get home at one in the morning the next day. I only got two to three hours of sleep a night for the first two weeks. It was such a brutal schedule.

Exhausted all the time, each day I had to make sure my uniform was perfect, no strings, and ironed. Just perfect. Then the training itself added a whole new level of difficulty. It was just unreal.

The Air Force Honor Guard's primary mission was to do funerals at Arlington National Cemetery in Washington DC. We would do on average six to eight funerals a day. Additional duties were working at the Pentagon as a tour guide, drill team, White House jobs, and other demanding yet rewarding activities. We had to prepare for the demanding climate and other things like standing at attention for long periods of time. My longest time standing at attention without moving was two hours and forty-five minutes. Talk about endurance!

I'll never forget my first job at the White House. We welcomed President Lee Myung-Bak from the Republic of Korea. Both he and President Obama gave speeches that were pretty long. It was a hot day on that White House lawn, when all of a sudden someone from the Coast Guard Honor Guard fell out. I mean, slap right on the grass. I wasn't going down, however. I was determined to stand tight and get through that tough day.

My patience got tested more than once. One time, we were in New York waiting for the President to arrive and give a speech. There were many world leaders at this event, and we were the cordon. The President was supposed to walk in between us as we presented arms. Well, he never came. I mean he did come, but they took him in through a different entrance and didn't tell us. So, we waited and waited, not moving for almost three hours when finally, someone let us know.

All of this training and duties were super hard, and I wanted to quit. Even being called by my country to serve the President wasn't enough to keep me motivated. I had no sleep, I was tired all the time, I was physically pushed to my limits, and I just didn't think I could do it.

Why-Power over Will-Power

What about my willpower, you might be thinking? I had willpower during my training and difficult presidential duties. I was motivated, determined, confident, and committed to my post. I had the drive and determination to succeed. I mean, that's why they selected me to try out. I had a lot of willpower.

But it wasn't enough.

See, the thing with willpower is that when obstacles come, challenges come, and life hits you hard and turns your world upside down, many would give up or fail completely. Willpower isn't strong enough to overcome these obstacles. But you give me someone with Why-power, that is when your willpower gets turbocharged. You will turn the world upside down to reach your destination, despite all of the obstacles and challenges.

It's like this. If I said there was a lion in a cage outside your house and I guaranteed you $1000 to go walk passed it, would you do it? Yeah, probably you'd say yes. Someone with willpower would. The lion is locked up, so that's an easy grand. But, let's say the cage was unlocked. That ups the stakes and changes the game. Now, there is a real obstacle that threatens your life. I don't care how determined you are and how confident you are - you are not going to go outside with an uncaged lion.

Now, let's change the game again. What if I told you that there was an uncaged lion outside? You can see it in your front yard, but you also see your kid or someone you love out there as well. Would you go out there and save them? Yes, you would! Not because of your willpower, but because of your why-power. Your why is so strong, that it doesn't matter if a lion is outside. You're going to go and get your kid!

When I went through that presidential training, it was a time when they were kicking people out of the military. They were downsizing and if I failed, I would be kicked out. The stakes were high, and the game was tough. But my why was stronger. See it wasn't willpower that got me up every day, it wasn't willpower that kept me going when I wanted to quit, it was my reason why.

My wife was pregnant with our first child. That was my why. They kept me going every day. I had no choice. I knew I had to succeed because I didn't want my family put on the street. I didn't want them to experience what I experienced growing up, living in shelters, in garages, and in storage units. I had a strong WHY, and there was nothing that was going to stop me from reaching my goal.

Having your 'why' keeps you focused on those goals you set and helps you overcome obstacles that arise on your way to your destination. That's the difference between those who succeed and those who quit. Is your why strong enough?

Spend some time thinking about what motivates you at the core. What's going to make you not give up? What's going to push you when you feel like throwing in the towel?

- Maybe it's a situation that you just can't go back to.

- Maybe it's just the thought of being average.

- Maybe it's the idea that you don't want to be another person in the cemetery who died with their potential still locked inside them.

- Maybe it's your loved one, your baby, your kids, or your family.

- Maybe it's something a mentor said that impacted you so much you've got to succeed.

You've got to figure this out for yourself. It's the key difference between those who can withstand the obstacles on the journey from potential to purpose – and those who can't.

I wasn't going to let any challenge or obstacle stop me from accomplishing my goal because my family was my WHY.

When your why gets bigger, then the how gets easier.

When faced with challenges and obstacles, when the many enemies surface to block you from reaching your destination, we all wonder HOW we will do it. Have you ever asked yourself that? How in the world am I going to do this? Well, when the why gets stronger, the how gets easier. The HOW becomes more clear. Now, it's not that a list suddenly comes to your mind. You don't all of a sudden get the steps on how to navigate around your roadblock to reach your destination. When your why gets stronger, you will just make it happen. Your why becomes so strong, that it doesn't matter how it gets done, it just gets done.

I have found that your why is one of the strongest secrets that will propel you towards your destination. It will unlock your potential. It has the power to pull you towards your vision. It will take you through this journey from potential to purpose.

It's not willpower – it's WHY-power. Find yours and become powerful.

CHAPTER SEVEN

The Power of Why

> *"When you feel like quitting think about why you started"*
>
> – Anonymous

Summary

How can you strengthen your 'why'?

Every purpose has a "why" behind it. The power of why will make you keep going when you want to give up because something inside you knows that if you don't fulfill your purpose, nothing else in life matters. So, the question to you is what exactly is your why?

Reflection

Reflect on the reasons behind your goals and dreams. Why are they important to you? How do they align with your values and purpose? Consider the moments when your 'why' has kept you motivated despite challenges. How can you strengthen your 'why'?

Actionable Steps:

It's time to take

1. **Discover Your Why:** Spend time journaling to uncover the deeper reasons behind your goals and aspirations.

2. **Create a Why Statement:** Write a powerful statement encapsulating your 'why' and place it somewhere visible.

3. **Reflect Regularly:** Revisit and reflect on your 'why' regularly to stay motivated and focused.

4. **Daily Reminder:** Set a daily reminder on your phone with your 'why' statement.

5. **Share Your Why:** Discuss your 'why' with a friend or mentor to reinforce your commitment.

Guided Exercise:

Purpose Reflection: Write a reflective essay on what drives you and why. Consider how your 'why' has influenced your past decisions and how it will guide your future actions.

Vision Board: Create a vision board that visually represents your 'why' and your goals. Include images, words, and quotes that inspire you.

Understanding and anchoring your 'why' provides the motivation and direction needed to pursue your goals with determination. As you continue this journey, the next chapter will delve into the vital role of faith in discovering and fulfilling your purpose, guiding you to align with a higher calling.

8
The Search

"It's not an accident that musicians become musicians and engineers become engineers: it's what they're born to do. If you can tune into your purpose and really align with it, setting goals so that your vision is an expression of that purpose, then life flows much more easily."

– Jack Canfield

In this book, we've put together a map for you to follow as you take your journey from potential to purpose. You find your 'why' in order to boost up your willpower and keep yourself motivated along the journey to accomplishing your goals as you fight the many enemies that come to limit you from reaching your potential. You take steps toward your goals and purpose that help you grow and become the person you need to be.

But, before we reach the final stage in the journey, there is one final piece of the puzzle I want to talk about:

Faith

My near-death experience in Iraq changed me. This entire book comes from that split-second moment. When you come that close to death, it changes you. You have a sense of urgency that you never had before. Even if you're as young as I was, you suddenly realize how incredibly short life is. It seemed like I had decades to live. But, when that bomb landed right next to me, those decades were reduced to seconds. I didn't have all kinds of time. I had less than the time it takes to blink.

But, the bomb didn't go off and I'm here. I was forever changed, though. I wanted to find out what my purpose was. I didn't want to die full of potential, but rather empty, having fulfilled my purpose. I didn't want to make the graveyard any more wealthy than it already was.

After my time in Iraq, I searched like crazy for what my purpose was. I was very motivated to find it. After coming close to death, I didn't want to die before discovering it. I reached out to many mentors for guidance and wisdom as I embarked on this new journey of discovery. However, I kept coming up short. I kept searching and kept failing.

I remember one winter I went to visit my in-laws in Florida and while there, I went to chat with one of my mentors, Jonathan Sansom. We called him Pastor J. I went on to share how I was stuck and needed help as to why I was created. What he said next changed everything for me.

Pastor J. told me, "Don't seek purpose. Rather, seek God, and purpose will find you."

This simple yet profound advice shifted my focus from a relentless pursuit of purpose to a deeper relationship with Jesus. Jesus said in Matthew 6:33, "But seek first His kingdom and His righteousness, and all these things will be given to you as well." This verse isn't just a command; it's a key to accessing the fullness of life that God has for us.

What Jesus is saying here is that our primary focus should be on pursuing the things of God's Kingdom—His values, His ways, and His presence. When we prioritize our relationship with Him and align our lives with His righteousness, everything else falls into place. It's not that our needs and desires are unimportant, but rather that they find their proper context and fulfillment when God is our first pursuit.

Seeking the Kingdom first means making God's will and His ways the priority in every area of our lives. It's about aligning our hearts with what He cares about, letting His priorities become our priorities. When we do this, we position ourselves under His provision and blessing. It's like tuning into the right frequency—when we're aligned with Heaven, Heaven's resources are released into our lives.

This doesn't mean we won't face challenges or that everything will be perfect. But it does mean that we can trust God to take care of our needs, knowing that He is a good Father who delights in providing for His children. It's about living with the confidence that as we pursue Him, everything we truly need will be taken care of in His timing and His way.

So, Matthew 6:33 is an invitation to trust, to shift our focus from earthly concerns to heavenly priorities, and to live in the assurance that God's ways are higher and better than ours. It's a call to live a life that seeks His Kingdom first, knowing that in doing so, we unlock the fullness of life that He has promised."

Faith became the cornerstone of my journey. It's through faith that I learned to trust the process, even when I couldn't see the entire picture. Faith isn't just about belief; it's about trust, surrender, and a deep connection with something greater than ourselves. It's about recognizing that there is a divine design for our lives and that our purpose is part of a grander plan.

As I deepened my faith in Jesus, I began to understand that my purpose wasn't something I needed to force into being. Instead, it was about being receptive to the divine guidance that was already present in my life. The more I sought to align myself with Jesus' teachings, the more my purpose became clear. As Proverbs 3:5-6 says, "Trust in the Lord with all your heart and lean not on your own understanding; in all your ways submit to Him, and He will make your paths straight."

Proverbs 3:5-6 is a profound invitation into a deeper relationship with God. The first part, 'Trust in the Lord with all your heart,' is a call to complete reliance on God. It's about surrendering every part of our lives to Him, not just the areas we find easy to give up. It's a reminder that trust isn't partial—it's wholehearted. This means that even when circumstances don't make sense or when we can't see the full picture, our confidence remains in God's goodness and faithfulness. 'Lean not on your own understanding' challenges us to move beyond our limited perspective. Human understanding is finite and often flawed, shaped by our experiences and perceptions. But God's wisdom is infinite and perfect. By choosing not to rely solely on our own reasoning, we open ourselves up to divine insight and revelation, trusting that God knows the best way forward, even when it defies our logic. The verse continues, 'In all your ways acknowledge Him.' This is about making God central in every aspect of our lives—our decisions, plans, and daily activities. Acknowledging God means seeking His will, honoring His presence, and inviting Him into every situation. It's about living with an awareness of His constant guidance and involvement in our lives.

Finally, the promise: 'He will make your paths straight.' When we trust in God, avoid leaning on our own understanding, and acknowledge Him in everything, He promises to direct our paths. This doesn't necessarily mean the path will be easy or without challenges, but it does mean it will be the right path. It will be a path that leads to His intended purpose for our lives, marked by His peace and provision.

In essence, Proverbs 3:5-6 teaches us that a life of faith isn't about having all the answers, but about trusting the One who does. It's about living in partnership with God, where we lean into His wisdom and let go of our need to control every outcome. It's a journey of trust, surrender, and continual seeking, knowing that as we do, God will lead us into His perfect will."

We often think we can map out our destiny with our own strength and wisdom, but without Jesus, we can never fully reach it. It's like trying to navigate through a dense forest without a compass. Jesus is that compass, guiding us through every twist and turn, helping us avoid pitfalls, and leading us to our true calling.

Discovering Your Purpose Through Faith

1. Surrender to the Process: Trust that there is a divine plan for your life. Surrendering means

letting go of the need to control every aspect and allowing your journey to unfold naturally. As Jeremiah 29:11 assures us, "For I know the plans I have for you," declares the Lord, "plans to prosper you and not to harm you, plans to give you hope and a future."

2. Seek Divine Guidance: Spend time in prayer, meditation, and reading the Bible to connect with God. This connection will provide clarity and direction. In James 1:5, we are encouraged, "If any of you lacks wisdom, you should ask God, who gives generously to all without finding fault, and it will be given to you."

3. Listen to Your Inner Voice: Your intuition is a powerful tool. When aligned with your faith in Jesus, it can guide you toward your purpose. Pay attention to the signs and messages you receive, trusting that God is

leading you. John 10:27 says, "My sheep listen to my voice; I know them, and they follow me."

4. Embrace Patience: The journey to discovering your purpose may take time. Be patient with yourself and the process. Trust that everything is happening in God's perfect timing. As Ecclesiastes 3:1 states, "There is a time for everything, and a season for every activity under the heavens."

5. Stay Committed to Growth: Personal and spiritual growth go hand in hand. Continue to work on yourself, developing your character and abilities. This growth will prepare you for the fulfillment of your purpose. Philippians 1:6 encourages us, "being confident of this, that He who began a good work in you will carry it on to completion until the day of Christ Jesus."

When you seek Jesus first, everything else falls into place. Your purpose is not a separate entity but an integral part of your spiritual journey. It is through faith that you find the strength to overcome obstacles, the courage to face challenges, and the wisdom to navigate your path.

Faith doesn't eliminate the difficulties you will face, but it equips you to handle them. It gives you the resilience to keep moving forward, even when the road is tough. It provides you with a sense of peace and assurance that you are on the right path, even when you can't see the entire journey ahead.

As you continue your journey from potential to purpose, remember that your faith is your greatest ally. It will sustain you, guide you, and empower you to achieve your goals. Your purpose is not just about what you do but who you become in the process.

The search for purpose is not a destination but a journey. It is a path filled with growth, challenges, and discoveries. As you navigate this journey, let your faith be your compass, guiding you toward the fulfillment of your divine purpose.

Remember, you are not alone. You have Jesus guiding you, a community of support, and a purpose within you waiting to be unleashed. Embrace the journey with an open heart, a willing spirit, and unwavering faith.

Your potential is immense, your purpose is profound, and your journey is just beginning. Seek Jesus, embrace your faith, and let your purpose unfold. The world is waiting for you to shine.

It's time to unlock your potential and live your purpose.

CHAPTER EIGHT

The Search

> *"Don't seek purpose. Rather, seek God, and purpose will find you."*
>
> Pastor Jonathon Sansom

Summary

How has seeking Jesus influenced your sense of purpose?

So, none of this matters if you don't have a relationship with God first. But why? Because everything in creation was created with a purpose from the birds to the trees to mankind. As God created each individual, He created them with a purpose. Your voice, your ethnicity, your gifts, your talent, "the hand you were dealt," and everything else all play into God's purpose for your life. Before you can truly know your purpose, you have to know God, so that He can reveal to you everything in you, heal you from the things that hurt or hindered you, and change your perspective on how you see yourself. God wants to be a Father to you through intimacy so that you can reflect your created purpose in the earth. This will help you in business and in your personal life. Spending alone time with Him and reading His word allows you to learn of yourself and Him, so that everything else will make sense.

Reflection

Reflect on the role of faith in your journey towards discovering your purpose. How has your relationship with God influenced your decisions and direction in life? Consider moments when you felt closest to understanding your purpose. How did your faith play a role in these moments? How can trusting God and seeking His will help you navigate uncertainty and challenges in your journey?

Actionable Steps:

It's time to take

1. Daily Devotion Time: Set aside time each day for prayer and reflection, focusing on deepening your relationship with God. Use this time to seek His guidance and wisdom for your life's purpose.

2. Scripture Meditation: Choose key scriptures such as Matthew 6:33 and Proverbs 3:5-6 to meditate on throughout the week. Reflect on how these verses apply to your current life situation and write down any insights.

3. Journal Your Faith Journey: Start a journal dedicated to your faith journey. Document your prayers, reflections, and any revelations you receive about your purpose. This can help you track your spiritual growth and see how God is guiding you.

4. Surrender Exercise: Identify areas of your life where you may be leaning on your own understanding or struggling to trust God fully. Write these down and consciously surrender them to God, asking for His direction and peace.

5. Seek Community Support: Engage with a faith community or find a spiritual mentor who can support and guide you in your journey. Share your reflections and seek wisdom from others who are also committed to living out their divine purpose.

6. Act on Faith: Identify one area where you can step out in faith this week. This might be pursuing a new opportunity, volunteering, or simply trusting God with a challenging situation. Take this step with confidence, knowing that your actions are aligned with seeking God's will.

7. Reflection and Review: At the end of each week, review your journal entries and reflect on how God has been speaking to you. Consider how your faith has grown and how you can continue to trust in God's plan for your life.

These steps are designed to help you actively engage with your faith, deepen your relationship with God, and align your actions with your divine purpose. Remember, the journey to discovering your purpose is as much about who you are becoming as it is about what you do.

Beyond The Blueprint

As we reach the culmination of "Unveiling The Blueprint: A Transformative Journey From Potential To Purpose," let's pause and reflect on the incredible journey we've undertaken together. This book isn't merely a collection of thoughts and exercises; it's a living, breathing guide designed to ignite your potential and align you with your divine purpose.

The path from potential to purpose is a sacred pilgrimage, one of self-discovery, growth, and transformation. We've dug deep into the treasure troves within us, set clear and actionable goals, and embraced the mindset shifts necessary for true change. We've confronted the fears that hold us captive, renounced the joy-killing habit of comparison, and found strength in the power of a compelling 'why.'

Faith, as we've explored, is not just a component of this journey—it's the foundation. Aligning with Jesus brings clarity and courage, enabling us to face life's challenges with unwavering resolve. It's this spiritual alignment that keeps us anchored, ensuring that we're not just drifting through life but moving purposefully toward our destiny.

As you step forward, remember, this book is the starting point, not the destination. Real transformation comes from daily application and intentional living. Dive deep into the actionable steps, fully engage in the guided exercises, and let reflection become a daily practice. These practices will not only solidify your understanding but also integrate these truths into the very fabric of your life.

Embrace this journey with an open heart and a fearless spirit. Let the wisdom gleaned here guide you through life's complexities, steering you toward a life rich in purpose and fulfillment. Your potential is boundless, and your purpose is uniquely yours. By continually seeking to understand and manifest this purpose, you'll not only transform your life but also impact the world around you in profound ways.

Thank you for embarking on this journey with me. May "Unveiling The Blueprint" be your enduring companion and source of inspiration as you explore and fulfill your divine purpose. Remember, the blueprint of your life is in your hands—go forth and build a future that radiates passion, purpose, and profound impact. The world is eagerly waiting for you to step into your greatness.

Next Steps:

To continue growing and transforming, consider these next steps:

1. Join a Community: Surround yourself with a tribe of like-minded people who are also on this journey of discovery and purpose. Community is essential for growth.

2. Ongoing Learning: Don't stop here. Invest in your personal and spiritual development by attending workshops, seminars, or enrolling in courses that resonate with your goals.

3. Reflect and Adjust: Make it a habit to regularly review your goals and reflect on your progress. Adjust your course as necessary to stay aligned with your purpose.

4. Personal Coaching: If you're looking for personalized guidance, consider the value of

having a coach. Scan the QR code below to explore one-on-one coaching opportunities with Andre Butler. A coach can provide you with tailored advice, accountability, and strategies to unlock your full potential and achieve your divine purpose.

These next steps are your call to action. Embrace them and continue building a life that not only fulfills you but also inspires and empowers others. Your journey is unique, and the path you choose will not only transform your life but also make a lasting impact on the world. Let's walk this path together—toward a life filled with purpose, passion, and boundless possibilities.

THE POWER OF IDENTITY

ANDRE BUTLER

ANDRE BUTLER

Made in the USA
Columbia, SC
04 November 2024